nature's baby animals

BABY ANIMALS
OF THE SEASHORE

Carmen Bredeson

Dennis L. Claussen, PhD, *Series Science Consultant* Professor of Zoology, Miami University, Oxford, Ohio

Allan A. De Fina, PhD, ***Series Literacy Consultant*** Dean, College of Education/Department of Literacy Education, New Jersey City University, Past President of the New Jersey Reading Association

CONTENTS

WORDS TO KNOW

blubber (BLUH bur)—
Layer of fat under the skin of some animals.

hatchling (HACH ling)—
A baby born from an egg.

larva (LAR vuh)—
The early part of some animals' lives, such as shrimp and crabs.

THE SEASHORE

Seashores are places where the ocean meets the land. Seashores might have sand, rocks, ice, or mud. Baby animals have special ways to stay safe and live at the seashore.

BABY
HARBOR SEAL

A harbor seal pup can swim right after it is born. The pup follows its mother into the water. Sometimes a pup cannot find its mother. The little seal calls her with a MAAAAA sound.

A horseshoe crab starts out in the water as a larva. Then it grows into a tiny crab with a hard shell. Horseshoe crabs look like little tanks. Their long tails help them move around in the water.

BABY HORSESHOE CRAB

BABY WALRUS

A baby walrus is called a calf.

A baby walrus is born on the ice. It rides on its mother's back in the cold water. The walrus has thick blubber under its skin. The blubber keeps the walrus warm.

Baby saltwater crocodiles tap out of their eggs. The mother carries her babies in her mouth. She takes them to water. The babies slide into the water. They are ready to swim.

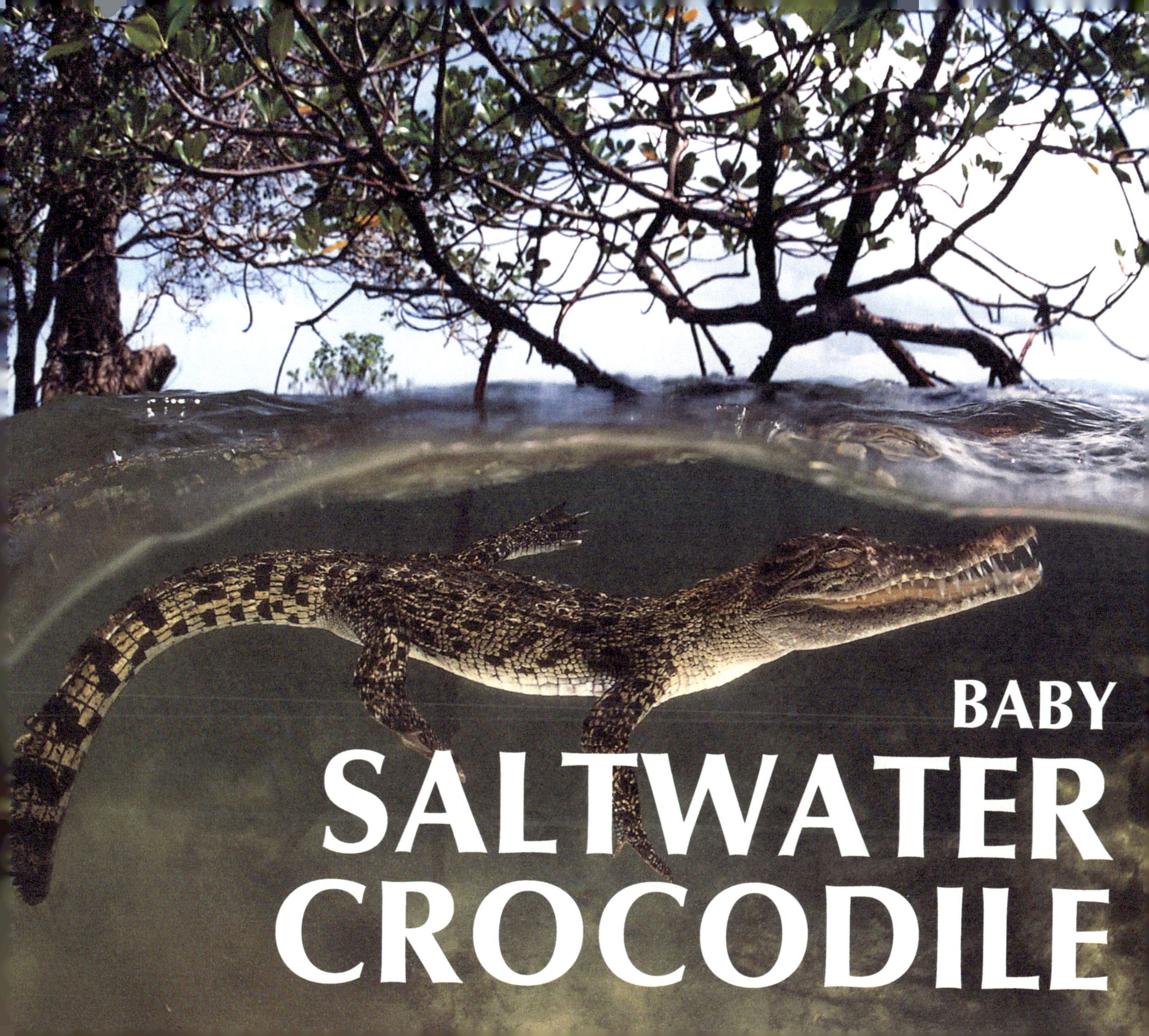

BABY SALTWATER CROCODILE

BABY HERRING GULL

Herring gull chicks call PEEP, PEEP, PEEP. Their mother and father bring food to the hungry babies. Herring gulls eat fish, crabs, and garbage left on the beach. They help keep the beach clean.

This chick sits on the feet of its mother or father. It rests against the thick feathers to stay warm. The parents take turns hunting for food. They bring fish for the chick to eat.

King penguin chicks grow brown feathers after they hatch.

BABY KING PENGUIN

BABY SEA OTTER

Sea otter pups are born in the water. The mother swims on her back. The pups ride on her belly. Soon the pups learn to swim and hunt.

Little green sea turtles hatch from eggs. They run across the sand. They splash into the water. The hatchlings hide in seaweed until they grow bigger. They eat small crabs and fish that live in the seaweed.

BABY GREEN SEA TURTLE

Learn More

Books

Himmelman, John. Who's at the Seashore? Minnetonka, Minn.: NorthWord Press, 2009.

Kaufman, Gabriel. Saltwater Crocodile: The World's Biggest Reptile. New York: Bearport Publishing, 2007.

Lockwood, Sophie. Sea Otters. Mankato, Minn.: Child's World, 2006.

Sexton, Colleen. Seal Pups. Minneapolis: Bellwether Media, 2008.

Web Sites

Monterey Bay Aquarium. Fun and Learning.
<http://www.montereybayaquarium.org/lc/kids_place>

NOAA. Ocean Explorer.
<http://oceanexplorer.noaa.gov/gallery/livingocean/livingocean.html>

INDEX

~For Kate and Caroline, our beautiful granddaughters~

Enslow Elementary, an imprint of Enslow Publishers, Inc.
Enslow Elementary® is a registered trademark of Enslow Publishers, Inc.

Library of Congress Cataloging-in-Publication Data

Bredeson, Carmen.
Baby animals of the seashore / Carmen Bredeson.
p. cm. — (Nature's baby animals)
Includes bibliographical references and index.
Summary: "Up-close photos and information about baby animals of the seashore"—Provided by publisher.
ISBN 978-0-7660-3565-2
1. Seashore animals—Infancy—Juvenile literature. I. Title.
QL122.2.B742 2011
591.769'9—dc22
2009037901

Paperback ISBN: 978-1-59845-226-6

Printed in the United States of America

102010 Lake Book Manufacturing, Inc., Melrose Park, IL

10 9 8 7 6 5 4 3 2 1

Photo Credits: © Alan and Linda Detrick/Photo Researchers, Inc., pp. 2 (right), 14; Bill Raften/Photolibrary/Getty Images, pp. 2 (left) 18; © Fred Bavendam/Minden Pictures, pp. 3 (bottom), 8, 9; Hiroya Minakuchi/Minden Pictures/Getty Images, p. 16; Manoj Shah/The Image Bank/Getty Images, pp. 1, 21; Lynn M. Stone/Nature Picture Library/Getty Images, p. 19; M. Watson/Science Source, p. 20; Michael Quinton/Minden Pictures/Getty Images, pp. 15, 23; © Paul Nicklen/Getty Images, pp. 3 (top), 10, 11; Shutterstock, pp. 5, 7; Suzi Eszterhas/Minden Pictures/Getty Images, p. 6; Dhana Kencana/Anadolu Agency/Getty Images, pp. 3 (middle), 12; WILDLIFE GmbH/Alamy Stock Photo, p. 13; © Yva Momatiuk & John Eastcott/Minden Pictures, p. 17.

Cover Photo: Manoj Shah/The Image Bank/Getty Images

Note to Parents and Teachers: The Nature's Baby Animals series supports the National Science Education Standards for K–4 science. The Words to Know section introduces subject-specific vocabulary words, including pronunciation and definitions. Early readers may need help with these new words.

Enslow Elementary
an imprint of
Enslow Publishers, Inc.
40 Industrial Road
Box 398
Berkeley Heights, NJ 07922
USA
http://www.enslow.com